To

....

From

....

....

For Juliet, Isaac, and Alexander J.S.

Text by Christina Goodings
Illustrations copyright © 2017 Jamie Smith
This edition copyright © 2017 Lion Hudson

The right of Jamie Smith to be identified as the illustrator of this work has been asserted
by him in accordance with the Copyright, Designs and Patents Act 1988.

Published by Lion Children's Books
an imprint of
Lion Hudson plc
Wilkinson House, Jordan Hill Road,
Oxford OX2 8DR, England
www.lionhudson.com/lionchildrens

ISBN 978 0 7459 6553 6

First edition 2017

Acknowledgments
Bible extracts are taken or adapted from the Good News Bible © 1994 published
by the Bible Societies/HarperCollins Publishers Ltd UK, Good News Bible ©
American Bible Society 1966, 1971, 1976, 1992. Used with permission.

A catalogue record for this book is available from the British Library

Printed and bound in China, December 2016, LH06

The Lion
Easy-read
Bible

Retold by Christina Goodings
Illustrated by Jamie Smith

LION
CHILDREN'S

Contents

In the Beginning

Genesis 1

The children had gathered around the fire. A gust of wind sent sparks into the night.

"Listen," said the storyteller. "In the beginning there was nothing: just a great darkness... and God.

"God said, 'Let there be light,' and there was. And the light was good.

"That was the first day. On the days that came after, God called the world into being: land and sea and sky; sun and moon and stars...

"... And every plant that grows, every fish that swims, every bird that flies..."

"Or waddles," said a child.

"Or runs," said another.

"And all the animals with their amazing patterns and their wild and wonderful calls," said the storyteller.

"Then God made people," the storyteller said.
"Everything in this world is for you to care for and
to enjoy.

"On the seventh day God rested... and from the very beginning, God has told us that every seventh day should be a day of rest."

The Garden of Eden

Genesis 2–3

God planted a wonderful garden in Eden. It was a good and lovely place. The first man, Adam, had all he needed.

But he was lonely.

God made a woman to be his friend and companion.
The first woman was Eve. They loved one another and
were happy.

One day, Eve heard a whisper.

"Why not eat this lovely fruit?" asked a snake.

"God has told us never to touch it," replied Eve. "It is the one thing we must not do. If we eat it, we will die."

"I don't believe that," said the snake. "It will make you wise.

"It's just that God doesn't want you to be wise.

"Try some. It's good."

Eve was tempted. She ate the fruit.

She shared the fruit with Adam.

Suddenly they both saw everything differently.

They felt ashamed to be naked, so they made clothes.

That evening, God came and found them.

"You have disobeyed me," said God. "Now you cannot stay in the garden.

"You must go out into the wild world, where you will find good things and bad things."

Adam and Eve left the garden. At the entrance, God put an angel on guard. The angel's sword flashed in every direction. There was no way back.

From that time on, people had to work and work to make a living.

They tended the soil.

They kept flocks and herds.

Would they ever be friends with God again?

The Story of Noah

Genesis 6–9

As the years went by, the number of people grew.

The problem was, they became wicked. People always seemed to be fighting!

God saw there was just one good man: Noah.

"I am going to send a flood," God told him. "I am going to wash away this bad old world.

"I am choosing you to save just enough of the bad old world so it can begin again. First, build an ark...

"Take on board your family: your wife, your three sons, and their wives...

"and two of every kind of animal...
"and food to last many weeks," said God.

Then the rain came. For forty days and forty nights it rained. The world disappeared under the flood.

The ark floated on the water. Days and weeks and months went by, and still the world was flooded.

One day, the ark crunched into the ground.

"We're on a mountaintop," said Noah. "The flood must be going down."

After forty days, Noah sent out a raven to look for land. It flew away.

"Oh dear," said Noah. "I'll try again."

He sent out a dove. It came back with an olive leaf in its beak.

"That's good news," said Noah. "It's a sign the land is drying out."

At last it was time for everyone to leave the ark. The animals dashed away to make homes and have babies.

Noah and his family said thank-you prayers to God.
A rainbow spread across the sky.

"The rainbow is a sign of my promise," said God.
"I will never flood the world like that again.

"There will be summer and winter, seedtime and
harvest for ever."

The Tower of Babylon

Genesis 11

When the world was young, people all spoke the same language.

Together they made their home on the wide, flat plain of Babylonia. Together they discovered how to make mud bricks and build houses with them.

Then, together, they had a brilliant idea. "Let's build
a tower, higher than any other — one that will reach to
heaven. Then we'll be famous!"

They all worked together.

God saw what they were doing. "The people think too highly of themselves," said God.

"I will mix up their languages. They won't be able to work together. That will put a stop to their arrogant plans."

In no time at all, people were using different words. They couldn't plan anything together. They couldn't work together. So they all went their different ways. And the tower was just left to crumble.

Abraham and the Promise

Genesis 11–21

Among the descendants of Noah was a man named
Terah. He had grown up in the city of Ur, on the plain
of Babylonia. Then he made a plan to go and settle in
the land of Canaan.

He and his family set out boldly, but they got only as far as a place called Haran. "I will make my new home here," declared Terah.

God spoke to Terah's son Abram: "I want you to go on. Take your household to Canaan. Your family will become a great nation there."

Abram set out.

Under Canaan's starry skies, God made a promise: "Your family will one day be as many as the shining stars. All this land will be theirs.

"You will have a new name: Abraham, meaning 'father of nations'.

"Your wife's new name will be Sarah, meaning 'princess'," said God. "She will be the mother of those nations."

At long last, God's promise came true. Abraham and Sarah had a son. They were so happy! They named him "Isaac", which means "laughter".

Abraham and Isaac

Genesis 22

Abraham was very proud of his son, Isaac.

Then God spoke: "Abraham, take your son to a high mountain. Offer him as a sacrifice to me there."

Abraham went with Isaac. As he got ready to kill his own dear son, God spoke again:

"Stop! I don't want human sacrifice. All I want is your obedience.

"The nation that begins with you and Isaac will be as many as the stars in the sky and the grains of sand on the shore."

Jacob and Esau

Genesis 24–33

Isaac grew up and married Rebecca. They had twin sons: Esau was the firstborn and Jacob was second.

The two boys were not like one another.

Esau loved being outdoors and was good at hunting. His father admired him.

Jacob liked to stay at home, where his mother doted on him.

From when they were boys, Jacob was jealous of Esau. "Because he's just that tiny bit older," he fretted, "he'll get the best of everything when our father dies."

One day, Esau came home hungry.

"Can I have some of that bean soup you've made?" he asked Jacob.

"I'll swap it for the privileges you get as the elder son," snapped Jacob.

Esau agreed.

Sometime later, when Isaac was old and blind, he sent
Esau to go and hunt animals for a stew.

While Esau was gone, Jacob and Rebecca made goat
stew. Then Jacob dressed up so Isaac would mistake
him for Esau.

He took in the meal Isaac had asked for... and
received the blessing due the firstborn son.

When Esau came back, he was very angry at being
cheated. Jacob had to flee. As he slept under the stars,
he had a dream.

"I will give you all this land of Canaan," God told
him. "I will be with you and protect you always."

But for now he had to go and work for his uncle
Laban. As the years went by, Jacob bred his own
flocks and so become wealthy. He also married two of
Laban's daughters, Leah and Rachel.

In his heart he always knew that he belonged in
Canaan. One day he must return there with his family.

That meant meeting Esau again. As Jacob set out, he was afraid.

"Please God," he prayed. "Please don't let Esau destroy us all.

"Please keep my family safe. They are your people."

He made plans to shower Esau with rich gifts: sheep and goats, cows and camels and donkeys.

But Esau had forgiven him. The two brothers agreed
to live as neighbours and as friends.

Joseph and His Dreams

Genesis 37

Jacob had a large household, including twelve sons.
His favourites were the two sons of his wife Rachel.
They were Joseph and Benjamin.

One day, Jacob gave Joseph a beautiful and expensive cloak. It wasn't just clothing: it was a sign that Joseph was to be the next head of the household. The ten elder brothers were furious.

One night, Joseph had a dream. "We were gathering in the harvest," he said. "My sheaf stood up straight. Your sheaves all bowed down to it."

"Is that so?" sneered the brothers. "Don't start thinking we're ever going to bow down to you."

Joseph had another dream. Once again he told his family.

"In my dream, the sun, the moon, and eleven stars bowed down to me."

Even Jacob was angry at that. "Don't start thinking that your mother and I and your eleven brothers are going to bow down to you."

One day, the ten elder brothers were out looking after the flocks. Jacob sent Joseph to check that all was well.

They felt angry just seeing him in his fancy coat. "We could kill him out here!" they began to grumble.

Only Reuben disagreed.

  While Reuben was away, the others saw traders
passing by. They sold Joseph as a slave.

  "We can just tell our father a made-up story – about
finding a scrap of his cloak, covered in blood," they
agreed.

Joseph in Egypt

Genesis 39–46

Joseph became a slave in Egypt. He worked hard, but his owner's wife told lies about him and had him thrown into jail.

God gave him the wisdom to explain dreams. That helped him make friends.

One of those friends was set free. He went back to his old job as the king's butler. When the king had some puzzling dreams, the butler told him about Joseph.

The king sent for him.

The king told Joseph about his dreams.

"I saw seven fat cows," he said, "then seven thin cows that came and ate them up.

"After that I saw seven ears of grain, round and plump. Seven thin ears came and gobbled them up."

The king asked, "What do these dreams mean?"

"Both dreams mean the same thing," replied Joseph. "There will be seven years of good harvests, then seven years of bad harvests.

"You need to choose someone to store the extra from the good harvests to last through the lean years."

The king replied almost at once: "I choose you."

For seven years Joseph made sure that some of the
harvest grain was properly stored.

Then when the harvests failed, he was in charge of
sharing it out.

One day, ten men arrived from Canaan.

"Please let us buy food," they begged. They all bowed
down in front of the proud Egyptian.

Joseph recognized his elder brothers. But what of his father? And Benjamin?

When he found out Benjamin was still alive, he made a plan.

"One of you stays as a hostage," he said. "I want you to prove your story. Go and fetch that young brother."

The brothers went away with the grain they needed.
When it was all eaten up, they came back with
Benjamin. Joseph welcomed them with a feast. Then
he loaded their packs with more grain and sent them
home.

"Slip a silver cup into Benjamin's pack," he told his
servants.

As soon as the brothers were on their way home, Joseph sent his servants after them.

"Our master says you've stolen something!" they cried.

They searched the packs and found the cup.

"Our master wants the thief as his prisoner," they declared.

Everyone trooped back to Joseph. The brother named Judah stepped forward.

"Please don't keep Benjamin," he said. "The wife our father loved most had two sons. One is dead; Benjamin is the other. Keep me instead."

It was then that Joseph knew for sure: his brothers were sorry for what they had done so long ago.

"That brother isn't dead... I am Joseph!" he cried. "God has turned the wrong you did into something good!

"Go and fetch my father and all the household.

"Come to Egypt, and be safe."

The Baby in the Basket

Exodus 1–2

When Jacob and his family made their home in Egypt, they were one big household.

Years passed. There were children and grandchildren and great-grandchildren. The family became a nation.

The king of Egypt at that time knew nothing of
Joseph.

"Make these people work as slaves on the building
sites!" he ordered.

"And throw all newborn baby boys into the River
Nile."

One mother wove a basket and made it waterproof.
She floated her baby boy among the reeds of the river.
Her daughter Miriam waited and watched.

A princess of Egypt came to the river to bathe.
She saw the basket.
When her servants lifted the lid, they found the baby.
"Oh, the poor darling. I shall keep him as my son,"
she said.
"I'm going to name him 'Moses'."

Miriam stepped forward.

"I know someone who could look after him for you," she said.

"That would be helpful," said the princess.

Miriam fetched her mother. Baby Moses grew up safely with her. When he was old enough, he went to live in the palace with the princess.

Out of Egypt

Exodus 2–15

Moses grew up as a prince in Egypt.

He was angry to see how hard the slaves had to work.

One day, he was so angry he picked a fight with a slave-driver... and killed him.

In fear for his life, Moses fled to the wild country.
There he became a shepherd.

One day he saw a strange sight: a bush was on fire,
but not burning up. God spoke to Moses from the bush:
"I want you to go to the king of Egypt. Tell him to let
my people go."

Moses was afraid. "Throw down your stick," said God. Moses did so. It became a snake.

"Now pick it up," said God. As Moses did so, the snake became a stick again.

"I have done that to show my power will be with you, Moses," said God.

So Moses went back to Egypt, and, with his brother
Aaron, went to see the king.

"God says this: 'Let my people go'," they told him.
The king refused.

"You can be sure there will be trouble," warned Moses.

There was trouble, all kinds of things went wrong:
The River Nile turned blood red and the fish died.
Overnight, countless frogs came hopping into people's
homes – there were frogs everywhere. After that,
millions of gnats filled the skies, and then buzzing flies.

The animals died. People became covered with boils. Storms of hail flattened all the plants. A cloud of locusts flew in from the desert and ate every leaf and blade of grass. Then darkness fell across the land for three days.

Still the king of Egypt would not let Moses lead his people to freedom.

God told Moses what to do.

"The people must get ready to escape. They must mix their bread without yeast so it is quick to make and bake. They must prepare a farewell meal of lamb, and mark their doors with some of the blood.

"Death will pass over the houses marked with blood. It will strike all unmarked homes."

When that terrible disaster struck, the king gave in.
"Take your people away, for ever!" he ordered.

As the people set out for Canaan, the king changed his mind again. "After them!" he ordered his fighting men.

His army set out in chariots, driving the horses as fast as they could.

Moses and the people saw them. What could they do? They were at the edge of a sea.

Moses lifted his stick. God parted the waters and made a way through the sea so the people could escape.

Everyone sang songs of joy. Moses' sister Miriam danced and played the tambourine.

In the Wilderness

Exodus 15–17

Moses had led his people out of Egypt. "You are God's people," he told them, "the twelve tribes that belong to Jacob's family – the people of Israel."

But out in the wild country, the people soon became glum. "It was better in Egypt," they moaned. "We grew nice vegetables and everything."

"God will take care of us, even out here," Moses declared.

With God's help they found water to drink. Quails were easy to catch and good to eat. Flakes of manna collected on leaves overnight. They were crisp and sweet.

Laws to Live By

Exodus 19–30

One day, Moses went out alone to Mount Sinai. There God told Moses the laws and traditions that the people must obey.

Above all, they must love and trust their God alone.

They must also love one another, and be loyal, generous, and fair.

"This is my promise, my covenant," said God. "If the people keep my laws, then I will take care of them. They will be able to live in the land of Canaan in peace and safety."

The laws of the covenant – known as the Law – were written on two tablets of stone.

The Golden Calf

Exodus 32–34

Moses was away for some time. The people felt lost.

"We want another god, right here!" they told Aaron.

He used their gold earrings and necklaces to make an idol: a golden calf. They began to worship it.

Moses came back and heard the wild festivities.

"This is utterly wrong!" he cried, and he smashed the stone tablets of the Law.

He punished those who had led the people astray.

God helped Moses make a second set of tablets.

"We will make a golden box in which to treasure them," Moses told the people. "The ark of the covenant."

A Place of Worship

Exodus 35–40

Moses told the people God's instructions for how to worship him. They chose their best craftworkers and their finest materials to build a tent of worship – the tabernacle. The ark of the covenant was kept in the innermost room.

Priests were chosen to lead the people in worship.
Aaron was the first high priest. His breastplate bore
twelve jewels: each one a reminder that the twelve tribes
of Israel were dear to God.

Whenever the people looked toward the place of
worship, they knew for sure that God was with them.

Joshua

Deuteronomy 34; Joshua 1, 3, 6, 24

Moses had led his people out of Egypt, but he had grown old. God chose Joshua to lead them into Canaan. Joshua was a brave fighter. He was also obedient to God.

First, the people had to cross the River Jordan. Joshua told the priests to carry the ark of the covenant into the water. As they did so, the river slowed to a trickle. Everyone marched across.

They came to the city of Jericho. Soldiers looked down from the high city walls.

How could Joshua's fighting men take on such a well-defended city?

"Listen," said God to Joshua. "Carry the ark of the covenant around in a big procession: an advance guard, then seven priests, each with their trumpets, then the ark, then a rearguard. March around like this once for six days."

On the seventh day the procession set out again.
This time, they marched around the city seven times.
On a signal from Joshua, the priests blew their
trumpets, the people gave a shout...

... and the walls of Jericho fell down.
Joshua and his fighting force captured the city.

The capture of Jericho marked the beginning. With God's help, the people of Israel took control of all Canaan.

Joshua gave everyone a place to settle and make their home, tribe by tribe.

When Joshua was old, he called the people together.

"God has kept the promise: God has led us safely to this land, that we can call home.

"We must do what we promised: love God, worship God, and keep his laws.

"I and all my household promise to serve the Lord."

The people replied as one: "We too will serve the Lord."

A Time of Heroes

Judges 2

After Joshua died, the people of Israel forgot his example. They turned away from God and began to worship the local gods of Canaan. They believed them to have power over the weather and the harvests... but they were mistaken.

The peple of Israel didn't gain more control over their lives. They lost power as enemy nations attacked them and came to share their land.

Deborah

Judges 4–5

Even so, God sent strong leaders to rescue them. One of these was a wise woman named Deborah. She rallied a fighting force to defend the land against the Canaanite king Jabin. "We will fight on the banks of the River Kishon," she declared.

Jabin's commander Sisera set out with 900 chariots to defeat Deborah's forces.

God sent heavy rain. The ground became waterlogged and soft. The chariots got stuck. Deborah's fighting force won the day.

For many years, the people had peace.

Gideon

Judges 6–8

Once again the people of Israel turned away from obeying God's laws. God allowed the Midianites to harass them. They came at night, raiding the people's flocks.

Gideon was a young farmer, and he was terrified. He even decided to thresh his grain at night, in a place where no one would think of looking.

An angel appeared and said, "God is with you, brave and mighty man. You are the one who must rescue your people."

Gideon was bold enough to gather an army. Then he panicked.

"Please, God, give me a sign that I should go to war," he said. "I shall leave a fleece out on the ground overnight. If you want me to fight, make the fleece wet with dew, but the ground dry."

That is what he found.

"Oh dear," fretted Gideon. "Please, God – can you give me another sign? I shall do the same thing, only this time let the fleece be dry and the ground wet."

Gideon got the sign he wanted.

"You have gathered many men to fight," God told him, "but I don't want people to think that Israel won because of fighters. I want them to know that I defended them."

He told Gideon to send most of the army home, leaving just 300.

Gideon explained God's plan to the 300. They took up their places around the Midianite camp. Each had a blazing torch hidden in a pot, and a trumpet.

In the dark of night, on a signal from Gideon, they smashed the pots, waved the torches, and sounded the trumpets.

The Midianites awoke in a panic. They began fighting each other. Gideon and his army chased them out of the land.

Samson

Judges 13–16

Time and again the people of Israel forgot to obey their God. Time and again they suffered until some hero came to rescue them. Then there would be peace... for a while.

The Philistines, who lived down by the sea, saw their chance to harass the people of Israel.

Then God spoke to a couple who had no children. "You will have a son," said God. "You must dedicate him to me, and leave his hair uncut as a sign."

The child was Samson.

As a young man, Samson fell in love with a Philistine
girl. He wanted to marry her. At the wedding he
promised a big reward to anyone who could answer
a riddle.

His Philistine bride wheedled the answer from him.
She told her Philistine friends.

Samson felt tricked.

He began a one-man campaign against the Philistines.
He set fire to their harvest fields. He fought them with
whatever came to hand. He was so strong that they
could not stop him.

Samson fell in love again: with a Philistine woman named Delilah.

The Philistine kings made a plan: surely she could find out what made Samson so strong?

She pleaded and pleaded... until Samson told her.

"I am strong because I have been dedicated to God," he said.

"The sign of it is my uncut hair. If anyone cut my hair, I would be as weak as a baby."

Delilah told the Philistines.

She let them come to the house at night and cut Samson's hair. They made him their prisoner.

They blinded him and set him to work in the jail, turning the giant millstones. All the while, his hair was growing.

One day, they held a festival in the temple. It was a riotous event.

"Let's fetch our old enemy Samson and make fun of him," they laughed.

Samson was led to a place in the temple between two pillars. He reached out... and pushed them apart.

In his final act, he destroyed many of his people's enemies.

Ruth

Ruth 1–4

When Naomi was a young woman, she lived in Bethlehem with her husband and two sons. All was well until the harvests failed. Desperate to survive, the family went to the land of Moab.

There the sons grew up. Each married a Moabite girl.
Life had turned out well for Naomi. She hoped to
become a grandmother.

Then her husband and sons died.

"I shall go back to Bethlehem," she told her daughters-in-law. "You are young. You could marry again. So stay here among your own people."

One agreed, but the other pleaded to stay with Naomi.

"I want to be one of your people," said Ruth. "I will worship your God."

Back in Bethlehem, Ruth worked hard to take care of Naomi. She went gleaning for stalks of grain left in the harvest fields.

The farmer was Boaz. "Take care of that woman," he told his servants.

In fact, Boaz wanted to marry Ruth. When he found
out that Ruth wanted to marry him too, he was
delighted.

Ruth and Boaz got married. They had a baby son.
Naomi held the little boy close. She had had many
years of worry and happiness. Now she had a family
again. At long last, she was a grandmother.

Samuel

1 Samuel 1–3

Years had passed since the people of Israel had left the wilderness and made their home in Canaan.

They still treasured the tent of worship – the tabernacle – where the ark of the covenant was kept.

Now it stood in Shiloh. People came there for the big festivals.

One year, a woman named Hannah came to the
festival with her husband and prayed a tearful prayer:
"O God, please may I have a baby!

"If I do, I will bring him here, to be your servant
always."

God answered Hannah's prayer. Her little child was
Samuel. She brought him to Shiloh to help the priest,
Eli.

One of Samuel's jobs was to sleep in the tabernacle.
That way he could make sure the lamps burned safely
through the night.

One night, he heard someone calling his name.

"Samuel! Samuel!"

Samuel jumped up and ran to Eli. "Here I am," he said.
"But I didn't call you," said Eli. "Go back to bed."
The same thing happened again, and again.
Eli understood. "It must be God who is calling," he said.

When Samuel heard the voice again, he replied as Eli had told him:

"I am listening, God. I am ready to do what you ask."

"I have chosen you to be in charge when Eli dies," said God. "I have chosen you to be the next leader of Israel."

The First King of Israel

1 Samuel 4–9

The people of Israel were often attacked by enemy
nations. While Eli was still the priest in Shiloh, the
Philistines attacked. Eli let the Israelites take the ark
of the covenant into battle. They hoped it would bring
victory.

Instead, it was captured by the Philistines. Eli fell over and died when he heard the dreadful news.

The Philistines did not keep the ark for long. They claimed it had brought one disaster after another. They sent it back on an ox cart.

It ended up at a place not far from Jerusalem and there the ark stayed, in an ordinary house.

Samuel became the leader of the nation, just as God had said. For twenty years he gave wise advice.

But the people grew worried: who would defend the nation if he died?

"We want a king, just like other nations," they told him.

Samuel was dismayed. "It is not you they have rejected," God told him. "It's me they don't trust. I will show you who to choose as king."

The choice was a handsome young man named Saul.

Samuel and Saul

1 Samuel 10–16

Saul turned out to be an able soldier. He gathered an army and began defeating his people's enemies.

But he grew too bold. He stopped listening to Samuel's advice.

God spoke to Samuel again. "I will show you who to choose to be the next king," he said.

The choice was a shepherd boy from Bethlehem: David, son of Jesse.

David and Goliath

1 Samuel 17

King Saul needed good soldiers in his army. Among them were the elder sons of a man from Bethlehem named Jesse.

The youngest son, David, stayed at home, looking after the sheep.

One day, he went to the army camp with a basket
of homemade food for his brothers. While he was there,
he heard a mighty roar from the enemy's side.

"Listen to Goliath," the brothers explained. "He's
the Philistine champion. If anyone beats him, we win
the war. But who wants to die?"

"I'll fight him!" said David.

News of this boast reached King Saul. He sent for
David.

"You can't fight Goliath," said Saul. "You're just a boy.
He's been a fighter for years."

"I've killed wild animals that came hunting my sheep,"
said David. "If God can help me do that, God can help
me win."

David set out with his shepherd's stick and his
shepherd's sling. He stopped by a stream to pick up
five stones. They would be his weapons.

Goliath jeered at David.

"Are you going to beat me up with your stick? Do you think I'm a dog?"

"I'm going to beat you because the God of Israel is with me," cried David.

He fitted a stone to his sling. He whirled the sling and THREW.

The stone hit Goliath. He fell down heavily.
David won the victory.

Jerusalem

1 Samuel 18–31; 2 Samuel 1–7

David's victory over Goliath made him a national hero. King Saul became very jealous of him. His own son Jonathan saw that David was in danger.

"My father wants to kill you," he warned. "You will have to go into hiding."

For many years David was forced to live as an outlaw. Yet he never tried to harm Saul; instead he tried to defend his people.

Then came sad news: the Philistines had killed both Saul and Jonathan in battle. David knew his time had come.

He gathered his supporters around him and claimed the throne. The supporters of King Saul's family tried to stop David, but he was too clever and too strong. In the end, all the people of Israel accepted him as king.

David captured a hilltop fort and made it his city: a place from which he would rule the nation. He named his city "Jerusalem".

He set up a tent of worship in his new city. In a noisy procession, he had the ark of the covenant brought to it.

"God is the one who has saved our people," he declared. "Jerusalem is where we will worship him."

But David still had many struggles to face before his kingdom was at peace.

God spoke to him. "It is not you who will build the place of worship," said God. "It will be the next king, your son Solomon."

The Temple in Jerusalem

1 Kings 2–8

It cost a lot to build a temple. Solomon ordered the finest materials: stone, wood, gold, and bronze. He hired the finest craftworkers.

When it was finished, Solomon ordered all the leaders of all the tribes to Jerusalem.

The ark of the covenant was carried to the innermost room.

Solomon said a prayer:

"Let us praise God, who has given us peace.

"May God always watch over us.

"And may we live as God's people should, and keep God's laws and commandments."

The Divided Kingdom

1 Kings 11–12

As a young king, Solomon had asked God for wisdom. As he grew older, he was tempted by riches. He turned away from God. He made his people pay taxes to pay for his luxuries.

When he died, the people asked his son Rehoboam to be kinder. Rehoboam said no. Only the tribe of Judah accepted him. The other tribes made a man named Jeroboam king in a new kingdom named Israel.

God's kingdom was divided.

Ahab and Elijah

1 Kings 16–19, 22

The kings of Israel did not care much about God's laws.
The worst of them was named Ahab. He married a
foreign princess, Jezebel, and built a temple for her god,
Baal.

Only the prophet Elijah dared to challenge him.
"God will punish you," he told Ahab. "There will be no
rain for two or three years."

Elijah turned on his heel and went off into the
wilderness.

In the third year with no rain, Elijah came back.
"You have disobeyed the God of Israel," he warned.
"Now bring the prophets of Baal to Mount Carmel.
There we will hold a contest.

"We will build an altar. Your prophets must ask Baal to light the wood." The prophets prayed and danced and raved. But no fire came.

"Oh dear," said Elijah. "It seems that Baal is sleeping. Now pour water all over the altar."

When all the wood was soaked, Elijah prayed to God.
Fire came down from heaven and set it all ablaze.

"Take those false prophets and punish them," cried
Elijah.

"Now go," said Elijah to Ahab. "The rain is coming."

Ahab became more respectful of God, but his wife Jezebel was as selfish and wicked as ever.

Some time later, Ahab died in battle. The kingdom went to his sons, who chose to worship Baal as their mother Jezebel did.

Elijah and Elisha

1 Kings 19; 2 Kings 2

After the contest on Mount Carmel, Elijah went off into the wild country.

There, alone, in wild weather, God spoke to him in a quiet whisper.

"Go to a man named Elisha. I have chosen him to be the next prophet in Israel."

Elijah did as God instructed. Then, when his work on earth was done, he asked Elisha to come with him on one last journey.

As they walked, a fiery chariot came and swept Elijah up to heaven.

Jehu's Rebellion

2 Kings 9

Elisha remembered all that Elijah had told him. He showed everyone that he was God's prophet by the miracles he worked. Then came the time when he went to talk to a young army officer named Jehu.

"God has chosen you to overthrow the royal family and declare yourself king of Israel," he said.

Jehu set off in his chariot.

He reached the palace. Queen Jezebel stood at a window, her servants around her.

"Who is on my side?" he called. "Throw the wicked queen down."

Jezebel fell to her death. Jehu swept to power. "Under my rule, we will worship our own God," he declared.

The Enemy from the North

2 Kings 11–17

Even Jehu struggled to stay loyal to God all the time. The kings of Israel that came after him were even worse.

And all the while, in the kingdom of Judah there were good kings and bad kings.

God allowed a fierce enemy to invade the land: the Assyrians had the finest weapons and the swiftest chariots of war.

The northern kingdom of Israel was utterly defeated.
The people were led away, and others were allowed
to settle there. These people became known as the
Samaritans.

King Hezekiah of Judah

2 Kings 18–19

The mighty Assyrian army had defeated Israel. Then the emperor Sennacherib himself tried to attack the cities of Judah. From Jerusalem King Hezekiah sent a desperate message: "Please stop! I will pay whatever you demand."

Sennacherib demanded silver and gold. Hezekiah had to strip the precious metals from the Temple.

But Sennacherib and his army marched closer and surrounded the city.

Three messengers arrived at the city walls: "Give in!" they cried. "Accept our offer of peace, or expect the worst."

Hezekiah went to the prophet named Isaiah for advice.
"Don't be afraid," said Isaiah. "Sennacherib will leave
for his own country without even starting a battle."

In the night, the angel of death passed over the
Assyrian camp. Sennacherib awoke to a disaster scene.
He gave the order for everyone else to go home.

The Promise of a King

Isaiah 9

In the midst of all these troubles, the prophets brought good news.

"One day," they said, "God will send our people a king like David. He will be called 'Wonderful Counsellor, Mighty God, Eternal Father, Prince of Peace'.

"His kingdom will always be at peace. He will rule with justice until the end of time.

"God will make this happen."

King Josiah

2 Kings 20–23

Hezekiah's son and grandson in turn became kings of Judah. Neither of them obeyed God. Then, when he was just a boy of eight, Hezekiah's great-grandson Josiah became king. From the beginning he tried to obey God.

When he was a young man, he decided to have repairs done to the Temple. The builders set to work. In the upheaval, they found a book of the Law.

"This could be important," said the priest. "I must tell the king."

Josiah listened as the book was read aloud. He shook his head in dismay.

"There are so many laws we have forgotten," he cried. "We must work harder at making sure the people worship our God alone.

"And we must celebrate the Passover, as Moses first instructed. We must remember the night when God sent disaster to the Egyptians so our people could go free.

"It is a festival our people must never forget."

The Fall of Jerusalem

2 Kings 25

Under Josiah's rule, the people of Judah knew God's laws and obeyed them. However, enemies all around continued to harass the nation. To the north, King Nebuchadnezzar of Babylon defeated the Assyrians and swept south.

One king of Judah after another tried to resist. Their efforts were wasted.

In time the Babylonian army besieged Jerusalem. When they captured it, they burned the Temple.

The ark of the covenant disappeared. It was never seen again.

Far from Home

2 Kings 25; Psalm 137

Many of the people of Judah were taken from their homes to live in Babylon. They lamented the loss of the Temple and the city of Jerusalem.

To continue their traditions, the people of Judah – the Jews – began to meet each week, on the sabbath day of rest. Those who were wise taught them the stories of days gone by and the laws God had given them.

These meetings on the riverbank in Babylon were the first synagogues.

The Fiery Furnace

Daniel 3

The Babylonians were not cruel to the Jews. Some trained for jobs in King Nebuchadnezzar's government. Shadrach, Meshach, and Abednego shone at their work.

One day the king had a huge statue made. He ordered everyone to come and admire it.

"When the orchestra plays," cried a herald, "everyone must bow down to the statue.

"Anyone who refuses will be thrown into a fiery furnace."

The music began. Shadrach, Meshach, and Abednego did not bow down.

"We will only worship our God," they told the king.

Nebuchadnezzar flew into a rage. "Tie them up and throw them into the furnace," he cried.

The king watched as the flames licked around them...
but why were the men walking... and was that an angel
in there with them?

"Bring those men out of the furnace," he ordered.
"Their God is the greatest of all the gods."

And he gave them the most important jobs in Babylon.

Daniel in the Court
of King Darius

Daniel 6

Daniel was highly regarded in the royal court. He became an advisor first to Nebuchadnezzar, then his son Belshazzar, and after that to the Persian ruler who overthrew Belshazzar: King Darius.

The other advisors were jealous of Daniel's power. Some went to the king.

"You must make sure your subjects are loyal," they said. "Make a new law: say that anyone who doesn't put all their trust in you must be thrown to the lions."

King Darius was flattered and made the law. The men
went to spy on Daniel. They knew they would find him
facing in the direction of Jerusalem and saying prayers
to his God.

They dragged him to the king.

"Oh, the law wasn't about Daniel," said the king.
"I know he's loyal."

"But your law must be obeyed," said the men. "If you
let anyone off, all kinds of people will start disobeying."

Darius had no choice. Daniel was thrown to the lions.

The next morning he went to see what had happened.

"Are you alright?" he called.

"I am," replied Daniel. "God sent an angel to protect me."

"Pull that man to safety," ordered Darius. "Daniel's God is the greatest of all gods.

"As for those evil men who tried to get rid of him... now they must face the punishment."

The Promise

Ezekiel 34

Ezekiel was one of the Jews who had been taken
to Babylon. He was a prophet, and he brought this
message to the people.

"God says this: I am the shepherd of my people.

"My flock has been scattered; but I will bring them back home... to the mountains and streams of their land of Israel, and the pleasant green pastures."

The people dreamed of the time when his words would come true.

The Homecoming

Ezra; Nehemiah

When Cyrus of Persia came to power, he gave a new order: that the people of Judah who lived in exile could go back to their homeland.

The work was hard, and the people were often discouraged. Other people had been settled in their land, and they mocked the Jews as they tried to rebuild their city.

Nehemiah gave up his job in the court of the Persian emperor to go and help his people. He came up with a plan to get the city walls rebuilt. The people were encouraged and rebuilt the other towns and cities as well.

Ezra was a priest. He ordered everyone to come to Jerusalem. There he read aloud from the book of the Law, so everyone would know how to live as God's people.

Ezra also found out that Moses had told the people always to remember the years when the nation lived in tents in the wilderness. They were to build shelters of branches and live in them for one week. "We too must celebrate the festival of Shelters," he announced. The festival was celebrated for the first time since Joshua.

The Story of Jonah

Jonah 1–4

Ezra the priest was very strict. "We Jews should be different from other nations," he told people. "Jews should only marry Jews."

Did God care about the other nations? The story of Jonah set people thinking.

There was once a prophet named Jonah.

"Go to Nineveh," God told him. It was the city of the Assyrians. "Tell the people to stop being wicked, or they will be punished."

Jonah didn't want to help the people of Nineveh.
He ran away from the task, by getting on a boat
bound for far away.

A huge storm blew up.

"Help," cried the sailors.

Jonah had to confess. "The storm is my fault. I'm running away from God. Throw me into the sea."

As Jonah sank into the deep, the storm stopped.

God sent a big fishy something to swallow Jonah.
It took him to shore.

Jonah hurried to Nineveh.

"Stop being wicked," he cried. "Or God will punish you."

The people of Nineveh changed their ways. No
punishment came.

That made Jonah angry. He sat in a little shelter and sulked. Everything had gone wrong. Even the plant that shaded him had died.

"I see you care about the plant," said God. "Well, I care about the people of Nineveh."

Esther

Esther 1–9

Esther was the wife of King Xerxes, the ruler of Persia.

Now she was on a mission. Her uncle Mordecai had warned her that the king's advisor Haman planned to massacre all the Jews in the empire.

"You are Jewish and the only one who can plead for us," was Mordecai's message.

Esther looked at herself in the mirror and tried to
smile.

"You look lovely," said her maid.

"I need to," mumbled Esther. "The king chose me for
my beauty. But dare I go to him unbidden? It is a crime
for anyone to do that!"

Full of fear, she went to the king as he sat on his throne.
At last he spoke. "What do you want, Queen Esther?"
"I would like to invite you to a banquet," she said.
"You and your chief advisor, Haman."

The king was delighted to come.

So was Haman. "Now even the queen can see how important I am," he told himself.

That evening, all Esther asked for was a second banquet.

It was another wonderful evening.

"Tell me what you want, Queen Esther, and you shall have it," declared the king.

"I ask that my people be allowed to live," replied Esther. "That man Haman is a villain who wants us dead!"

King Xerxes was furious. He had Haman put to death and told the Jews they had the right to defend themselves from anyone who tried to harm them.

From that time on, the Jews have remembered this story at the festival of Purim.

Jews and Romans

Zechariah 9; Luke 1–2

Back in their homeland, the Jewish people learned to treasure their traditions. A prophet named Zechariah encouraged them to rebuild the Temple.

"One day, God will send a new king to Jerusalem — a king of peace, riding on a donkey," he said.

But the years went by and no king came. Other, more powerful, nations ruled the land: first the Greeks, then the Romans.

One day, the Roman emperor Augustus announced a census. "I need to know who lives in my empire so I can make them pay tax," he said.

At that time Mary was a young woman in Nazareth.
An angel came with a message from God. "God has
chosen you to be the mother of his Son. You will
name him Jesus."

"I will do as God wants," said Mary.

Joseph was planning to marry Mary. An angel spoke to him in a dream.

"Don't worry that Mary is expecting a baby before she is married to you. It is God's child, and God wants you to take care of him and Mary," said the angel. Joseph made a plan.

He went to Mary.

"I have to go to my hometown of Bethlehem for the census," he said. "I want us to be family — so let's go together."

They set out.

When they reached Bethlehem, the town was crowded. There were no rooms in the inn.

They took shelter in a stable. There, Mary's baby was born.

On the hills nearby, shepherds were out with their
sheep. They needed to protect them from night-time
dangers.

Suddenly, an angel appeared. "Good news," said the angel. "Tonight, in Bethlehem, a baby has been born. He is God's long-promised king.

"You will find him wrapped in swaddling clothes and lying in a manger."

Then the sky was filled with angels singing praises to God.

When the sky was dark again, the shepherds left their
sheep and hurried to Bethlehem.

They found Mary and Joseph and the baby, Jesus,
just as the angel had said.

Mary smiled as she listened to their story. Her child
really was as special as the angel had told her.

All the while, from far away, wise men came riding. They had seen a new star in the night sky.

"It is a sign that a king has been born to the Jews," they agreed. "We must go and worship him."

They went first to the city of Jerusalem. The only king
they found there was Herod. He wasn't really a king,
for he took his orders from the Roman emperor. Even
so, he was angry to think that a rival had been born.

His own wise men gave their advice.

"One of the prophets of long ago said this... that God's promised king will be born in Bethlehem.

"You could send the stargazers there."

"I will," thought Herod. "And I'll ask them to bring back news of any king."

As the men journeyed the few miles between Jerusalem and Bethlehem, the star led the way.

It hung low over one particular house. Inside the men found Mary and Jesus.

They presented their tribute gifts: gold, frankincense, and myrrh.

In a dream, an angel warned the men not to go back
to Herod. They chose a different road home.

An angel also warned Joseph that Herod might send
soldiers to find the child that might be king. Joseph took
his family to Egypt.

Jesus Grows Up

Luke 2

In time, Joseph took his family back home to Nazareth.
There Jesus learned to be a carpenter, like Joseph.

He also went to school and the synagogue. The
teacher – the rabbi – taught his pupils how to read.
They learned the old stories about their people and their
God. They learned the laws. They learned the sayings
of the prophets.

Every year, Mary and Joseph went from Nazareth on the trip to Jerusalem, to celebrate the Passover at the Temple there. When Jesus was twelve, he went with them.

But he wasn't with the group that set out for home. Frantic with worry, Mary and Joseph searched Jerusalem.

They found Jesus in the Temple courtyard talking to the rabbis.

"Why were you worried?" said Jesus to his mother. "This Temple is my Father's house."

Then he went home. He grew up a good and obedient son.

John the Baptist

Matthew 3

Jesus' cousin John had become a preacher. He lived in the wild country and dressed like a prophet of olden times. "Get ready to be part of God's kingdom," he preached. "Repent of your wicked ways and live as God wants."

Those who wanted to make a change he baptized in the River Jordan.

One day Jesus came and asked to be baptized.

"You don't have anything to repent of," protested John.

Jesus insisted.

As John lifted him out of the water, Jesus saw a dove flutter down to him from heaven. He heard a voice: "This is my own dear Son, and I am pleased with him."

The Choice

Luke 4

Jesus knew that God had a special plan for his life: to call people into God's kingdom.

He went off into the wild country alone, without food, to think and pray.

The Devil came and tried to change his mind.

"If you're so special to God, you could do anything," said the Devil.

"You could make these stones turn to bread."

"I've read the Scriptures," replied Jesus, "and I know that's not God's way."

There was nothing the Devil could say to tempt Jesus away from the path he had chosen.

The Preacher of Galilee

Luke 4–5

It was a sabbath day — the day of rest, when everyone met at the synagogue. Back in Nazareth, Jesus read aloud from the Scriptures.

"The spirit of the Lord is upon me, because he has chosen me to bring good news to the poor...

"To announce that the time has come when God will save his people.

"Today," said Jesus, "those words are coming true."
The people of Nazareth were angry.
"How can the son of Joseph be a prophet?" they said.
Jesus walked away: over the hills to Lake Galilee.

Jesus began going to the synagogue in the lakeside town of Capernaum. He was asked to give a talk.

A man started screaming at him.

"I know who you are: you're God's holy messenger," he yelled.

Jesus saw that the man was in the grip of some evil power.

"Leave him alone!" he commanded.

At once the man was well.

There was a fisherman in Capernaum named Simon.
When the synagogue meeting was over, he invited
Jesus to his home for a meal.

Simon's mother-in-law was in the house, sick with
fever.

With just a touch, Jesus healed her.

Sunset marked the end of the sabbath. From all over town people came to Jesus, bringing friends and relatives who were unwell.

Jesus healed them all.

Soon people were talking about Jesus all over Galilee.

Crowds wanted to see him and to listen to him.

One day, the shore was so crowded that Jesus asked to preach from Simon's boat.

When he had finished, he told Simon to push the boat out further.

"You and the other fishermen: let down your nets," he said.

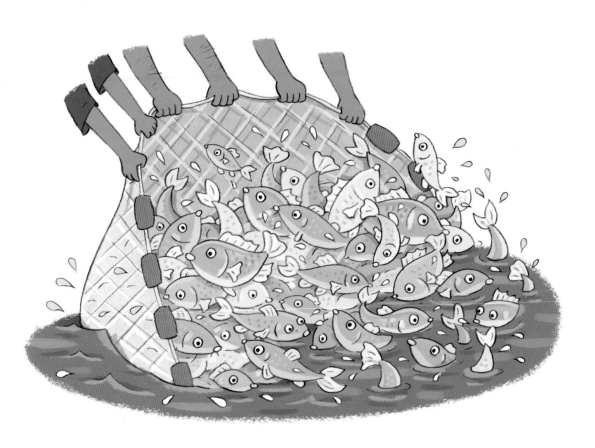

By a miracle, they brought in a huge catch of fish.

"Come with me, and you will be bringing people into God's kingdom," said Jesus.

Simon, Andrew, James, and John left their nets to follow him.

The Hole in the Roof

Luke 5

Jesus soon became known as a teacher – a rabbi. Other rabbis wanted to hear what he had to say. So did the people who thought of themselves as very religious: the Pharisees. One day, Jesus was in a house crammed full of such people.

Four friends arrived outside. They were carrying a
friend who could not walk, hoping Jesus could heal him.
They could not even get in the door.
They went up the outdoors staircase to the flat roof.

They made a hole in the roof and lowered their friend down on ropes tied to his sleeping mat.

Jesus smiled. "Your sins are forgiven," he said to the man.

"OH DEAR!" said the rabbis and the Pharisees. "Only God can forgive sins."

"But I have the right to speak on behalf of God," said
Jesus. "Watch this."

He turned to the man lying on the floor.

"Get up, pick up your bed, and go home," he said.

The man obeyed. He was completely cured.

Friends and Enemies

Luke 5, 6

In Jesus' day, no one liked tax collectors.

They took money from ordinary people to hand over to the Roman emperor. That was bad enough.

Worse, the tax collectors often took more than was right... and kept the extra for themselves.

One day, Jesus saw a tax collector named Levi.

"Come and follow me," said Jesus. Levi went at once.

The rabbis and the Pharisees complained. "It's wrong to mix with outcasts," they said.

"I haven't come to call respectable people back to God," Jesus replied. "I have come to help those who need to change their lives around."

One day, on the sabbath day of rest, Jesus went to a synagogue.

There was a man there who had lost the use of an arm. Jesus called him to the front.

The rabbis and the Pharisees watched and frowned. What was Jesus going to do?

"What does the Law say people can do on the sabbath?" asked Jesus. "Is it right to help, or to harm?"

Then he spoke to the man. "Stretch out your arm."

By a miracle, he was healed. The rabbis and the Pharisees were angry.

Jesus needed friends as well as enemies. He chose twelve
people to be his close disciples.

There were the fishermen: Simon — whom he
nicknamed Peter — and his brother Andrew;

James and his brother John;

... then Philip, Bartholomew, Matthew, Thomas, another James, another Simon, Judas...

... and another Judas: Judas Iscariot. Jesus trusted Judas Iscariot to look after the money for the group. But could he really be trusted?

Jesus the Teacher

Matthew 5–7

Wherever Jesus went, crowds came to listen to him. He told them how to live as God's friends.

"You must love one another," he told them. "It's not enough to be kind to your friends. You must love your enemies too.

"Imagine that one of the Roman soldiers asks you to carry his pack. The rules are you have to carry it one mile. Go the extra mile, and carry it for two!

"Don't say long and difficult prayers. Don't stand up
to pray where someone will see you.

"Go to a quiet place and say this:

Our Father in heaven:

May your holy name be honoured.

May your kingdom come.

May your will be done on earth as in heaven.

Give us the food we need each day.

Forgive us the wrongs we have done,
  as we forgive those who have wronged us.

Keep us safe from hard times
  so we are not lured away by evil.

"Make it your aim to live as God's friends, in God's kingdom. Stop fretting about money and how to get it. "Look at the birds: God feeds them.

"Look at the flowers: God clothes them.

"If God takes care of the birds and flowers, you can be sure God will take care of you.

"If you listen to my teaching and obey it, you are wise...

"... like the builder who built his house high on a rock. When the rain came and the wind blew and the flood rose, his house was safe.

"If you do not obey my teaching, you are foolish...

"... like the builder who built his house down on the sandy riverbank. When the rain came and the wind blew and the flood rose, his house fell flat."

Jesus and the Roman Officer

Luke 7

Jesus' power to work miracles made him the talk of Galilee.

One day, in Capernaum, a Roman officer came up to him.

"Please help me: my servant is ill. Can you heal him?"

"I'll come at once," replied Jesus.

"You don't have to," said the officer. "I'm a soldier and used to obeying orders and giving orders. I believe that you can give the order and my servant will be well."

"You have greater faith than my own people," said Jesus.

That very moment, the man's servant was healed.

Jesus and the Storm

Mark 4

One evening, Jesus and his disciples got into a boat,
to sail across Lake Galilee. Jesus was tired, and he fell
asleep.

During the night, a fierce storm blew up. The disciples
were very afraid.

"Wake up and help," they called to Jesus. "We're going
to die!"

Jesus stood up in the boat.

"Be still," he said to the wind.

"Lie down," he said to the waves.

At once, all was still.

"Who can Jesus be, that he can do such things?" whispered the disciples.

Jesus and the Little Girl

Luke 8

One day, a man named Jairus flung himself at Jesus' feet. "Please help me," he wept. "My little girl is very, very ill."

Jesus set out with Jairus, but the crowds made the journey very slow.

A servant arrived. "It's too late," he whispered to Jairus. "Your daughter has died."

"Trust me," said Jesus calmly.

He went to the house. He sent away the people who had come to weep and mourn.

He went to where the girl lay still on her bed.

"Little girl, get up," he said. To the delight of both her parents, that is exactly what she did.

Jesus and the Great Crowd

Luke 9

One day, a huge crowd came to listen to Jesus. They stayed for many hours, until the sun was beginning to go down.

"It's time to let the people go," said the disciples. "They need to go and get some food."

"I want you to give them something," came the reply.

"We can't!" said the disciples. "There are 5,000 people here.

"The only food we have is five loaves and two fish. A young boy here brought them for himself, but he's happy to share."

"Tell the people to sit down," said Jesus.

Then he took the loaves and fish and said a thank-you prayer. He handed the food to his disciples to pass around.

There was enough for everyone.

When the meal was over, the disciples filled twelve baskets with the leftovers.

The Parable of the Sower

Matthew 13

Jesus often told stories. "Once," he said to the crowds, "a man went out to sow his field.

"Some seed fell on the path. The birds came and ate it up.

"Some seed fell on rocky ground. It sprouted, but it did not have a good root. When the days grew hot, it wilted.

"Some seed fell among thorns. It tried to grow, but the young plants were choked.

"Some seed fell on good soil. It grew and gave a good harvest."

The disciples were puzzled. "What does the story mean?" they asked.

"The seed is God's word," replied Jesus.

"The seed on the path stands for those who hear my teaching but let the Evil One snatch it away.

"The seed on the stony ground stands for those who hear my teaching and try to obey. They give up when things get tough.

"The seed among thorns stands for those who hear the teaching, but then they get busy with all kinds of other things.

"The seed on good soil stands for those who hear my teaching and obey it. They produce a harvest of good deeds."

The Good Samaritan

Luke 10

One day a rabbi came to Jesus. He had a question that
he hoped would trick Jesus and prove that he was not a
good and wise teacher.

"What must I do to win eternal life?" he asked.

"What do the holy books say?" answered Jesus.

"That's easy," said the rabbi. "They tell us to love God
with all our being, and love our neighbour as ourselves."

"Quite right," said Jesus. "I thought you'd know."

The rabbi was angry. He needed ANOTHER question now.

"Who is my neighbour?" he asked.

Jesus told a story.

"There was once a man who was going from Jerusalem to Jericho. On the way, robbers came and beat him up. They took all he had and left him for dead.

"A priest from the Temple in Jerusalem came by.
He saw the man, but hurried by on the other side.

"A helper from the Temple came by. He tiptoed close to look at the man. Then he hurried by.

"A Samaritan came by."

Everyone knew that Samaritans didn't ever go to the Temple in Jerusalem.

"He stopped," said Jesus. "He went and helped the injured man, and lifted him onto his donkey.

"He took the man to an inn. There, he did all he could to help him get well.

"The next day he had to travel on.

"'Here is money,' he said to the innkeeper. 'It is to pay for you to help the man until he is well. If it costs more, I'll pay you next time.'

"Now tell me," said Jesus to the rabbi, "who was a neighbour to the man?"

"The one who was kind to him," came the answer.

"Then you go and do the same," said Jesus.

The Rich Fool

Luke 12

Jesus told this story to warn people not to be greedy.

"There was once a farmer. His land gave wonderful harvests.

"'But where will I store all these crops?' he fretted.

"'I know,' he said, 'I'll build bigger barns. Then I'll have everything I need for the rest of my days.'

"He went to bed feeling very pleased with himself.

"Then God whispered, 'You fool! You are going to die tonight. Who will get your wealth then?'

"So remember," warned Jesus, "don't fret about money. Take care to do the things that make you rich in God's eyes."

The Lost Sheep

Luke 15

The rabbis and the Pharisees came to Jesus with a grumble. "You mix with the wrong sort of people," they said.

Jesus told a story: "Imagine you are a shepherd, and that you have one hundred sheep.

"Then one goes missing.

"You leave the ninety-nine and go to look for your lost sheep. When you find it, you carry it home.

"You call your neighbours: 'Come round for a party! I want to celebrate finding my sheep.'

"God is like that shepherd," said Jesus. "When a wrongdoer comes back to God, all the angels sing."

The Forgiving Father

Luke 15

"Once," said Jesus, "there was a man who had two sons. They all worked on the family farm.

"The younger son dreamed of a more exciting life. He went to his father. 'When you die, some of what you own will become mine. I want it now... in cash.'

"Sadly, the father agreed. The young man took his money and went to a country far away. There he spent recklessly on all kinds of expensive fun.

"He spent all he had. He needed to make money if he was even going to eat.

"He got a miserable job, looking after pigs. Even the pig food looked tempting, he was so hungry.

"'My father's servants live better than this,' he said. 'I shall go home and say sorry. I shall ask to work as a servant.'

"He was still some way off when his father saw him. The old man ran to greet his son. He hugged him with delight.

"'Come on!' he called to his servants. 'Get this young man ready for a party. We're going to celebrate.'

"The elder son was working in the fields. When he heard the music and dancing, he was surprised.

"'It's a party for your brother,' explained a servant. 'He's come home. Your father is thrilled.'

"The elder son was very angry.

"'Please come and join us,' pleaded the father. 'Everything I have is yours. But we have to be pleased. We thought your brother was dead, but look – he's alive!'"

The Pharisee and the Tax Collector

Luke 18

"One day," said Jesus, "two men went to the Temple to pray.

"The Pharisee stood away from everyone else and said this:

"'Thank you, God, that I am not like others. I am not greedy or dishonest. I know all your laws and I keep them... down to every little detail.'

286

"The tax collector stayed at the back of the crowd. He fell on his knees and said this:

"'O God, please have pity on me. I've messed up just about everything.'

"And do you know who went home a true friend of God?" Jesus asked his listeners. "The one who was humble."

Jesus and the Children

Luke 18

One day some mothers came to see Jesus.

"We've brought the children," they told the disciples. "We'd like Jesus to say a blessing for them."

The disciples shook their heads. "Jesus is far too busy for that!" they said.

Jesus overheard.

"I'm not too busy," he said. "Let the children come to me, and don't try to stop them. They are welcome in God's kingdom."

Jesus and Zacchaeus

Luke 19

No one in Jericho liked Zacchaeus. He was a tax collector and he overcharged people to make himself rich.

When Jesus came to Jericho, the crowds elbowed
Zacchaeus to the back. He was short and couldn't see
a thing. So he climbed a tree.

Jesus came along the road. He looked up and called to Zacchaeus. "Come down! I want to come to your house."

Zacchaeus hurried down. Someone wanted to come to his house for a meal! That was so exciting!

Whatever Jesus said made Zacchaeus think hard about his life. At the end of the meal, he stood up.

"I'm going to change my ways," he said. "I will repay four times what I took from those people I've cheated."

Jesus smiled. "I came to seek those who had lost their way and bring them back to God," he said.

Riding to Jerusalem

Matthew 21

It was time for the Passover festival.

"We will celebrate it in Jerusalem," Jesus told his disciples. "Please fetch a donkey for me to ride."

As Jesus rode into Jerusalem, the crowds began to cheer. "God bless the king!" they cried.

Some waved palm branches. Others laid their cloaks down for the donkey to walk over.

"This is all wrong!" muttered the rabbis and the Pharisees. "Jesus is letting his followers think he's God's chosen king... the Messiah, the Christ."

While the crowd cheered, they muttered and tutted.

Jesus in the Temple

Luke 19

Jesus went to the Temple. There was a festival market in the courtyard. It was noisy and bustling, and the traders were charging as much as they dared.

Jesus began to push the stalls over. Soon there was uproar.

"Go, get out of here," Jesus told the traders. "The Temple is a place for prayer. You have made it a den of thieves."

The rabbis went and muttered to the Temple priests.

"We have to get rid of him," they agreed. "But how can we catch him when he's so popular?"

The Trouble with Money

Mark 12; Matthew 26

Jesus and his disciples went to the Temple in Passover week. They saw wealthy people putting money in the collecting box. Then a poor widow came and gave two small coins.

"Look at that!" said Jesus. "The priests make everyone feel they have to give money to the Temple. They don't care that a poor woman has given all she had!"

Meanwhile, the disciple named Judas Iscariot went to
see the priests in secret.

"If you pay me, I'll help you catch Jesus," he said.

For thirty silver coins he agreed to betray his friend.

The Last Supper

Luke 22; 1 Corinthians 11

Jesus and his disciples gathered to share the Passover meal.

Jesus took the bread and shared it with them. "This is my body, broken for you," he said. "When you share a supper like this, do so in memory of me."

After supper he took the cup of wine. "This cup is God's new covenant, sealed with my blood," he said. "When you drink it, do so in memory of me."

As supper came to an end, Judas Iscariot slipped away.

Gethsemane

Matthew 26, 27

Jesus and his disciples went out of the city. They planned to sleep under the stars, in the olive grove of Gethsemane.

Jesus knew there was trouble ahead. "Please God," he prayed. "If it is possible, please save me. But if it is not possible, I will do as you want."

Out from the shadows came Judas Iscariot. He had
brought soldiers to arrest Jesus. Peter and the other
disciples could do nothing to defend their master. In fact,
they ran for safety as the soldiers marched Jesus away.

Almost at once, Judas felt ashamed of what he had
done. He went and hanged himself.

Condemned

Matthew 26–27

The priests put Jesus on trial. They asked him lots of questions, but they had already made up their mind. In the morning, they marched him to the Roman governor, Pontius Pilate.

"This man claims to be our king," they said. "That means trouble.

"We want him put to death."

Pilate was not convinced, but the priests had a crowd on their side.

"Crucify him!" they shouted.

Pilate let them have their way.

Crucified

Luke 23

It was Friday morning. Jesus was handed over to Roman soldiers.

They led him to the place of crucifixion... a hill just outside the city. There they nailed him to a cross.

As he grew weaker, Jesus said a prayer for his enemies:

"Father, forgive them. They don't know what they are doing."

And then Jesus died.

A man named Joseph went and asked to be allowed to take Jesus' body. Just as the sun was setting, he arranged for it to be laid in a tomb. Then the stone door was rolled shut.

A New Beginning

Luke 24; Acts 1

On the Sunday morning, some women went back to the tomb. They planned to wrap the body more carefully and to show their respect to their dear friend.

They found the door was rolled open.

Angels spoke to them:

"Why are you looking among the dead for someone who is alive? Jesus is not here: God has raised him to life."

In the hours and days that followed, Jesus appeared to his friends and disciples.

"I have done all that God wanted me to do," he said. "Soon I must go to heaven, to prepare a place for you.

"Here on earth, I want you to spread the news about my teaching and about God's kingdom.

"I want you to invite all the world to be my followers, and friends of God."

God's Holy Spirit

Acts 1–2

Forty days after he rose from the grave, Jesus was taken up into heaven.

First, he told the disciples to go and wait in Jerusalem.

Not long after came the festival of Pentecost. Jesus' followers were in a room together. Suddenly, they saw something like flames. They heard a noise like a strong wind. God's Holy Spirit had come to give all of them the courage and the words they needed to spread the news about God's kingdom.

Peter

Acts 2

The disciple named Peter had something to prove. On the night Jesus was arrested, he had let Jesus go to his trial alone. Now he was going to be brave and loyal.

He went out into the street in Jerusalem and began to preach.

"Here is amazing news," he said. "You had Jesus
put to death. God raised him to life. He is God's king:
Christ, the Messiah. He has opened the way back to
God.

"Anyone who turns away from wrongdoing can live
as God's friend, in God's kingdom."

Christians

Acts 7–28; Colossians 3

From all over the Roman empire, people believed the message that Jesus was the Christ. They were the first Christians.

Among them was Paul. He changed from being an enemy of the Christians to their bravest missionary.

"You are the people of God," he told the new Christians. "You must show compassion, kindness, humility, gentleness, and patience. Be ready to forgive one another, as God has forgiven you. And to all these things, add love.

"Remember that your real life is with Christ, in all the glory of heaven."

For Evermore

Revelation 21–22

The first Christians always tried to live good and peaceful lives. Even so, people were afraid of their new beliefs and often treated them as criminals.

"Don't lose heart," wrote a Christian named John. "One day, God will defeat all that is wrong.

"One day, Jesus will return. We will be part of a new heaven and new earth, free from sadness, tears, and pain.

"We will live as God's friends in his holy city: the new Jerusalem."